Think Daniela!

Written by
Rob Waring and **Maurice Jamall**

to break (broken)

to burn

to swim

to take a picture

a smell

bridge

camp

fire

heavy

orange juice

river

rope

sneakers

waterfall

In the story

 Daniela

 Gemma

 John

 Faye

 little girl

"I need a nice hot drink!" says Gemma to her friends, John and Daniela. She is tired, cold, and very wet. They are at Bear Mountain Camp for the weekend. They are coming back from a long walk.

Daniela sits down. "That was a long walk," says Daniela. "But it was fun," says her friend, John.

"Yes, I enjoyed it. But look at my sneakers," says Daniela. "They are so wet and dirty."

"Mine, too," says Gemma.

Daniela and her friends make a big camp fire. They all sit near the fire. Everybody takes off their wet sneakers. Daniela sees Gemma's sneakers are wet.
"Gemma's sneakers are wet. I'll put them next to the fire," thinks Daniela.
She puts her sneakers and Gemma's sneakers near the fire.

"Give me a blanket, please," says John's friend, Faye.
"I'm cold."
John gives his friend a blanket. Soon, they all feel
much better.
"What are we going to do next?" asks John.
Daniela says, "I think we're going to make lunch."
"Oh, great!" says Gemma. But she does not like
cooking. She hates it.

Suddenly, John smells something. "What's that strange smell?" asks John.

"I don't know. Is it you, John?" asks Faye.

"Very funny, Faye!" replies John. Faye laughs.

"No," says Gemma. "You're right. What *is* that smell?"

Gemma looks at the fire. "Oh no! Quick. The sneakers!" she cries.

Gemma and Daniela's sneakers are burning!

Faye gets some water and puts it on the sneakers.
"Who put the sneakers near the fire?" asks Gemma. She is angry.
Daniela says quietly, "Umm . . . It was me. I'm sorry."
"Really! Daniela! You should be more careful," says Gemma
angrily.
"I'm really sorry, Gemma," says Daniela. "I'll be more careful.
I'll buy you some new ones."

Later, Mrs. Brown, their teacher from school, comes to speak to them.

"Right, everybody," says Mrs. Brown. "It's time to make lunch."

"Oh no," says John. "I hate cooking."

"Me too," says Gemma. "I don't want to cook, Mrs. Brown."

"No. You will *all* learn to cook. Come on," says the teacher.

Daniela puts the things on the table and the others start to make lunch.

Gemma and Faye make the lunch. They take the food to the table. John gets the drinks. Daniela wants to help because the others were angry with her before.

She says, "Can I help?"

John remembers the burning sneakers. He says, "No thanks, Daniela. It's okay."

"Please. I want to help," says Daniela. "I'll take the drinks to the table. Please!"

"Okay, but the juice is heavy," says John. "Be careful."

"I'll be okay. You go and sit down. I'll bring the drinks," says Daniela.

Daniela is happy. She thinks, "Great! John said I can help. Maybe he's not angry with me."

John sits at the table. Daniela picks up the juice and carries it to the table. "The juice is heavy," she thinks. "But, I'll be okay."

But she does not see the rope. She falls and the orange juice goes all over John and the food.

"Oh no!" thinks Daniela. "The juice!"

John is angry with Daniela. He looks at her.
"Daniela!" shouts John. "What *are* you doing?"
"I'm sorry, John," says Daniela. "I'm really sorry."
"I told you to be careful," he says. "And now look
at me. I'm all wet again."
Daniela says, "Yes, I'm sorry. I know. I was just
trying to help!"

"What were you thinking, Daniela?" asks Gemma. "You burned the sneakers and then you put the juice all over John."

"I was trying to help," says Daniela.

"Well, stop helping!" says John angrily. "When you help, you just make more trouble!"

Daniela sees a picture of a big bear. She thinks, "I must be careful. There are bears here. I must think!"

Later, Daniela walks through the camp. She thinks about the sneakers and the jugs. "Why do I do those things?" she thinks. "I must be more careful. And now my friends are angry with me. Well, not *all* my friends. Faye isn't angry with me."

Daniela decides to go and see Faye. "I need to talk to Faye," she thinks. "She won't be angry with me."

Daniela walks to the girls' cabin. "I should be careful,"
she thinks. "I must think more."
She goes to the door of the cabin. Then she sees a bear!
She is very surprised. It is behind her friend, Faye. But Faye
can't see it.
"Oh, no!" thinks Daniela. "A bear! It's going to hurt Faye!"
"I must do something," thinks Daniela. "What can I do?
Think Daniela!"

"Faye!" shouts Daniela. "Look out, Faye. Be careful!" Daniela runs to help Faye. "Faye, look out!" she shouts. "Run!"

Faye looks around at Daniela. She is frightened. She drops her camera.

"What?" Faye says. She sees Daniela running to her. "Run away, Faye," Daniela shouts.

Then Daniela sees the bear. She stops shouting. It is not a real bear! "Oh!" she says. "It's not a bear! Oh!"

Faye says to Daniela, "What *are* you doing? What *were* you thinking? Look at my camera! You broke my camera."

"I'm sorry Faye, I thought . . . ," says Daniela.

"It's not a *real* bear, Daniela . . . ," says Faye.

Daniela looks at the bear. "Yes. I know now," Daniela says. "Sorry, Faye. I thought it was going to . . ."
Faye says, "Yes, I know. But now my camera's broken. You should think more carefully. Of course, this isn't a bear!"
"I'm sorry," Daniela says. "I thought the bear was going to hurt you, Faye."
"We were taking pictures, Daniela!" says Faye.

Daniela is very angry with herself. "Why do I always do the wrong things?" she thinks. "I can never do things the right way." She walks away. She starts to cry.

"But I did try and do something, and that's good," she thinks. "But I was wrong. And now *all* my friends are angry with me. Gemma's angry with me. John's angry with me. And now Faye! Nobody likes me!"

She is very sad. "I'm not going to help anybody any more!" she thinks.

Daniela walks down to a big river. Some small boys and girls are playing on an old bridge. Suddenly, she hears a noise.

A girl is on the bridge. She shouts, "Help!" She is very frightened. Daniela sees the rope on the bridge. It is breaking. The girl is going to fall in the water.

"The bridge's breaking!" the boy calls to Daniela. "She's going to fall in the river. She can't swim. Please help her!"

"What should I do?" she thinks. "I should help her, but I helped before and got into trouble. Will I make more trouble? What should I do?"

"I must help her," she thinks. "Think! Think, Daniela!"

Then she has an idea. The boy has a rope. She runs to the boy and takes the rope from him. "Give me that," she says.

The boy is very surprised. Daniela turns and runs away with the rope.

Then the boy looks at Daniela and shouts, "Hey! That's my rope. Give it back to me!"

Daniela does not listen. She runs down to the river.

"Hey, come back!" says the boy. He does not understand.

"What are you doing with my rope?" the boy shouts to Daniela.
The boy sees the girl in the river. He says, "Annie, be careful!"
Daniela finds a big tree and puts the rope on it. She can see the
little girl. The girl falls off the bridge and into the river.
"Help me!" she shouts. "I can't swim!"
Daniela is frightened, but she jumps in the water holding the
rope. She swims with the rope.

She puts the rope around another tree. The river pushes the little girl to the waterfall.

She shouts, "Help! Help! I can't swim!"

Daniela shouts to the girl in the river. "Take the rope! Take the rope! I'll get you."

The river is very fast. The little girl shouts again, "Help me! Help me! I can't swim!" The other boys cannot do anything.

"Look, she's going to go over that waterfall!" shouts the boy.

The little girl takes Daniela's rope. Daniela pulls very hard on the rope. She pulls the girl out of the fast river. The little girl is safe now. Daniela talks to the little girl. "Are you okay?" she asks.
"Yes. I'm okay now," she says. "Thank you."
"Good!" says Daniela.

Gemma, Faye, and John come down to the river. "What happened?" they ask. The boys tell them about Daniela and the rope.

"Daniela, that was very smart of you," Faye says. "It was very quick thinking."

"Yes. Good job, Daniela!" say John and Gemma. "We're sorry for being angry with you."

Daniela smiles. She is very happy. "That's okay," she says. "I saw the danger and I helped the girl. I did the right thing," she thinks. "And I have my friends back, too!"